My Call To
Spiritual
Freedom

Journey to a True Self-Image - Book 3

This book has been published under the supervision of Prophet Del Hall III and by F.U.N. Inc., the parent company of Guidance for a Better Life.

Edited by Joan Clickner, Lorraine Fortier, Del Hall IV, and Terry Kisner. Cover Images by romolotavani/shutterstock.com

Cover Design by Del Hall IV.

No part of this publication may be reproduced, stored in or introduced into a retrieval system, or transmitted, in any form or by any means (electronically, mechanical, photocopying, recording or otherwise), without the prior written permission of both the copyright owner and the publisher of this book. Re-selling through electronic outlets (like Amazon, Barnes and Noble or eBay) without permission of the publisher is illegal and punishable by law. The scanning, uploading, and distribution of this book via the Internet or via any other means without the permission of the publisher is illegal and punishable by law. Please purchase only authorized editions and do not participate in or encourage electronic piracy of copyrightable materials. Your support of the author's right is appreciated.

Copyright © 2017 F.U.N. Inc. All rights reserved.

ISBN: 978-1-947255-03-6

My Call To
Spiritual Freedom

Journey to a True Self-Image - Book 3

Nitasha K. Canine

ABOUT THE AUTHOR

Nitasha "Tash" Canine spent much of her life seeking answers to classic spiritual questions such as, "Who am I? What happens to me when I die? What is my true purpose, and what is truth?"

An adventurous spirit led her to try many paths and teachings. She had not found anything that felt "complete" until finally being led to Guidance for a Better Life. There, her thirst for truth and meaning was quenched. A blessed opportunity was offered to her and eventually she became a disciple of the current Prophet of God, Del Hall III.

During spiritual travel with Del a realization burst within her: all she had ever sought to know was God and His Love. By experiencing this for herself directly a sacred and eternal bond was revealed to her. A loving relationship with the Divine developed, which inspires her with each new sunrise.

Tash now lives close to the retreat center with her beautiful wife Shanna, their large cuddly dog, and two lovable cats. She marvels daily at how Del's teachings can transform one into a true lover of life. She enjoys outdoor activities of all kinds and works in the field of bodywork doing structural integration and sports therapy.

TABLE OF CONTENTS

Author's Invitation...................................... 1

1. Childhood Dreams................................ 5
2. First Recognition of God's Love............ 12
3. Early Years... 16
4. Seeking Truth...................................... 20
5. The Pursuit of Happiness..................... 24
6. Boxes and Labels................................ 29
7. My First Love...................................... 33
8. A Higher Love..................................... 40
9. Shanna's Dream.................................. 45
10. Guidance for a Better Life.................. 47
11. The Blue Star..................................... 59
12. My Blue Bead.................................... 64
13. A Wind of Change............................. 66

14. Moving from Maryland..................... 69

15. Breaking Out!...................................... 73

16. God's Chosen Prophet..................... 79

17. Surrender.. 82

18. A Healing HU................................... 90

19. Facing Fears.................................... 94

20. A Journey to Lemuria With Prophet.... 96

21. An Ancient and Sacred Promise........ 101

22. Getting Out of the Maze................. 106

23. Diamonds Made to Shine................ 110

Postscript... 113

Appendix

Guidance for a Better Life "Our Story"...123

    My Father's Journey (Del Hall III).......123

    My Son, Del Hall IV........................135

What is the Role of God's Prophet?..........139

HU - An Ancient Name for God..............147

Articles of Faith 149

Contact Information..............................163

Additional Reading................................164

Author's Invitation

I invite you to join me in a journey through time with my teacher and inner guide, Prophet Del Hall III. His willingness to share the teachings of God with me has changed my life for the better. It was a process that transformed me from living a life in hiding to living life openly and wholeheartedly. In writing this book I was blessed with many memories; remembrances of God's Love shared with me as a child and as an adult in this lifetime. I was also given remembrance of certain past lives and shown God's Love within those as well. I started my journey with an ember of hope that I would someday be free to be me, happy in my own skin, and know true love. God's Grace has blown into my life like a fresh wind igniting those embers to burn as bright as the sun on a summer day. It is my hope you too will recognize and be touched by the warmth of God's Love; a love which is with us in every detail of our lives.

One night I had a dream I was working my day job and my phone rang. The ringer was on silent and the only way I knew to look at my phone was from an inner nudge. The screen said, "Call from God." The smart phone had two options, a choice to accept the call or reject the call. I accepted the call as quickly as possible and then I woke up. As I lay in bed afterward I kept thinking, "God called me — wow." But what did this dream mean? I often ask for dreams to come to me in a way that I can easily understand them. I saw several meanings. Obviously I was being called by God for some purpose. The phone call suggested I was being offered a more personal and close relationship. The phone itself signified communication and perhaps a better understanding of God's Language.

Looking deeper I felt the dream symbolized what Del has been helping me work towards all the years I have had the privilege to attend his retreats. This was my call to spiritual freedom — a call to come home to God and an invitation to experience my true self, Soul. In the spirit of answering this call I have committed to living each day with an attitude of confident expectation that with Prophet and personal effort I can do all things God has called me to do.

The wisdom and spiritual experiences within this book are credited to God's Prophet. It is an honor to share them with you.

1

Childhood Dreams

It was the late 1970s and I was preparing for bed. The top bunk was mine and my younger brother Sky had the bottom bunk. Mom and Dad were in the room just beside ours. We all lived in a two-bedroom and one bath home in a country setting in Laurel, Maryland. Our room was dimly lit as we lay face up bolstered with pillows, each with something to engage our young minds. Sky's book was all about dinosaurs and mine was a National Geographic Magazine on ocean life. I marveled at the various species of fish and wondered what it might be like to someday swim in the ocean. I was six years old, drifting off to sleep quite peacefully as I normally did while looking at pictures in a book or magazine. Soon I found myself in a light spiritual body with the exact same physical features I had as a young girl. My shoulder-length brown curly hair and round face were the same. My eyes were blue and my small lean arms and legs looked the same, but I shimmered as if encased in a suit made of light. I floated through the ceiling in my light body and exited my house through the roof. I was in a dreamlike state but also consciously aware of what was happening while my physical body slept in the top bunk of my single bed. As I floated around the perimeter of our home I could see our brick rambler was painted white, and the front porch light was on.

The purple-flowered wisteria bushes offered a pleasant fragrance about the property. Colorful flowers adorned the perimeter of our house. I noticed our very large catalpa tree in the backyard and several dogwood trees off to the side of our home as I slowly floated in my spiritual body.

My father's garden was vibrant with tomatoes, cucumbers, zucchini, and other summer vegetables. The air was warm and humid around me and there were no other homes for miles. We lived on a government-owned property consisting of over three hundred fenced acres, which was part of the work arrangement my father had. For Sky and me this was a childhood wonderland. There were ponds, creeks, gravel roads to bike on, and plenty of woods for building forts.

My father was part of a program designed to bring back endangered species. His specialized work was with whooping cranes, the tallest North American bird. This and the sandhill crane are the only two species of crane found in North America. One of the bird areas was close enough to our house that I could hear the distinct whooping sound each day and night. It was always in the background — one constant in my changing young life. Still in a dream state I was testing my ability to control my flying skills. I flew just above the grass as fast as I could. It felt as though the thought of going from where I was to where I wanted to go was all I needed in this light spiritual body to get me there. I would think, "I want to go really fast," and I would be flying at exhilarating speeds. When I wanted to slow down I would think, "I want to slow down," and it would be so.

I flew over the cranes, and the full moon and stars gave me enough light that I could see their white feathers and red heads. Most of the birds would go inside their enclosures to sleep, and some would stay outside and gracefully move about the night as if patrolling. It looked like a bird security system. When I was done exploring I would think of my cozy bed and slip in through the rooftop to float effortlessly back into my physical body. If I had any trouble getting back into my body I would think of my big toe and usually this focus was all it took, and I would wake up in my bed. This was a huge blessing in my life at the time, which I did not appreciate because it happened so frequently and naturally I did not think it would ever go away. I am not sure why the ability to travel spiritually left me but a couple years later it did. I missed the freedom greatly and throughout my life hoped to do this again.

This is also around the time my parents started having difficulty in their marriage, and I recall feeling unsteady about my life. My parents were doing the best they could. My father was in his late twenties and my mother was a few years older. Each day we had homemade healthy food to eat and a clean and tidy environment to live in. Mom made sure of this as it was one of the main ways she expressed her love. We had a small kitchen where my mother spent much of her time looking out at us playing from the window as she prepared our meals. My father liked his work, but it seemed there was a growing tension. He would frequently come home frustrated. The higher paid college educated scientists Dad worked with would not consider his suggestions because; he said they thought he was not equal to them in intellect, which upset him. At least that is what I could gather from their fights. My father seemed to be smart and talented regardless of not finishing college. He was self-taught in many skills and was an amazing artist. I began to notice a change in the tone of my parents' voices towards each other as time went by. Their voices got louder and louder, screaming, breaking dishes, pushing each other, and sometimes my mother would end up crying. I could not understand why they were so angry with one another. I wanted to make everything better between them so I started trying to make them laugh.

I realized I could put on the Groucho Marx glasses someone had gifted me and make up jokes; and they would forget their troubles for a while. This brought me joy and seemed to help make them feel good too.

2

First Recognition of God's Love

My mother told me a couple stories of when I was young. She said that while she was seven months pregnant with me she tripped and began to fall down a steep flight of stairs. She said that as she was falling someone caught her and put her back on her feet. She described it feeling as real as a physical hand breaking her fall, but she could not see anything or anyone around. She did not know who it was but was sure of her experience. She surmised it must have been "God's Hand" that saved us. It spared her from injury and saved my life. She expressed that the impact of how she was falling probably would have killed me.

One day in her mid-twenties, shortly after giving birth to me, she walked the large farmhouse property she shared with several other couples. She held me close to her heart swaddled in my baby blanket. Her heart was heavy with worry, and she told me she asked God some questions: "How will I care for this child? Will You provide?" She told me a tiny voice from where she held me said, "He will." She said she looked at me and thought, "Where did that come from?" I was only a newborn baby and could not talk. She told me she thought God spoke to her that day reassuring her to trust in Him.

When I was six years old my Dad took my younger brother and me fishing. There was a pond on the property where we lived and he loved to fish on Friday evenings. One time he took us with him, and I recall the warm summer night like it was yesterday. My father was on one side of the pond and my brother and I were on the other. We were on a pier and I was intensely focused on grabbing one of the plants growing out of the pond called a cattail. These plants have brown fuzzy tops that look like a tail. I liked to play with real cat tails and these plants. I loved to twirl them in my fingers because it was soothing to me. I kept trying to grab one without falling into the water. I did not know how to swim but drowning was not on my mind. As I reached for the fuzzy top of the plant I lost my footing and fell into the water. I remember falling in and sinking down in slow motion. As I looked up toward the pier I could see the top of the water where the light of dusk broke. I was waiting to touch the bottom to push off and get back to the top. Sinking and sinking I began to yearn for a breath of air. Just when I thought I would run out of breath, a strong burst of energy pushed me up towards the top. I broke through the surface with such force I was able to grab onto the pier and pull myself up with ease. It was as if something pushed me up out of the water and put me safely onto the pier. I knew it was not my own effort that propelled me out of the water. Somehow, I was protected. I did not talk about it or understand what it meant, but I knew I could have drowned that evening had I not been saved. We did not attend church as a family, but I recall my mom sharing a prayer of protection with us. She said if we were ever in trouble to pray to God for help. I do not remember if I recited this prayer while I was sinking toward the bottom of the pond, but I was saved nonetheless.

3

Early Years

My mother was raised Catholic. She told us she did not want to subject us to her childhood experiences of religion which in her opinion was a lot of guilt, shame, and fear. Sitting in church was not something that interested me, so I was happy about her decision. One night everything changed and a heaviness entered my life which seemed to plague me off and on until I finally made peace with my past by God's Grace. I noticed my father's frustration reaching new heights, and he was drinking more heavily. Within the yelling and screaming between my parents were hurtful words, and I realized my father was addicted to alcohol. They would argue for hours, and finally my mother would give up telling him he was drunk. He would follow her around the house, and the yelling and screaming would continue into the night. I gasped at the sight of the two people I loved most in this world tearing each other apart. It seemed like nothing I could do would make it better anymore. I was somewhat shy but also developed an anxious nature as a child, which followed me like a shadow into adulthood. My parents' marriage grew more and more distant. Over the years I could not recall any pleasant memories anymore. It was as if the fights erased all the memories of my childhood for a while, even the good ones. Little did I know walls had formed around my heart. I was angry and hurt. And would stay this way for many years, unaware of its effects in my life.

When I attended first grade my mother would dress me up in frilly dresses and brush my long hair before I got on the bus. I was quite lovely as a little girl, however I wanted none of it. Before leaving for school I put pants in my backpack, and as soon as I got to school I took off my dress and put the pants on. All of my friends were boys, and I would not be caught dead with a doll or anything pink. I played sports of all kinds. My toys were footballs, play guns, and my bicycle. I even adapted a special walk from my cousin Vincent who was a bodybuilder. It looked like a cowboy who had dismounted a horse after a long journey.

One night I snuck into the kitchen drawer and completed my look. I took out my mom's scissors and cut my hair short. When I went to school the next day my first-grade teacher Ms. B. called my parents in for a talk. She warned them that if they did not do something I was going to end up a lesbian. Hearing this I knew whatever a "lesbian" was it did not sound good. I needed to find out how to stop this from happening. A seed was planted that how I was born, although transient from the big picture view of Soul, was unsavory. Something was wrong with me. Still, from the age of five until about thirteen I looked and acted like a boy.

4

Seeking Truth

For a while in middle school I went with a good friend to her Christian youth group and studied the Bible. What I had experienced of religion so far seemed incomplete, like important truths were missing. I could not help but wonder where was the part about living more than one life? Somehow I believed that we did. How could a loving God send His children to Hell for eternity? What I had experienced of religion seemed pretty restricting. It seemed like a lot of rules: do this and go to Heaven, do that and go to Hell. I felt like we had to do everything "right" or we would be rejected. I loved God and Jesus but did not sense I belonged in any orthodox religion so I kept searching. Over the years I learned a little about Far

Eastern teachings and macrobiotics which my parents followed but still had not found anything that felt complete.

When I got out of middle school and started high school I decided I needed to hide my sexuality so I could continue to have friends. My creed was "Don't be gay!" I did everything I could to make up for this perceived shortcoming. In high school I grew my hair long and began to wear make-up. By this time I did not feel like a boy stuck in a girl's body. I liked how I looked but did not really find boys attractive. I was asked to go to the movies, to parties, or to restaurants with guys, which I did so I could fit in. As I did this I could see hope springing up in my parents. Each time I would go on a date they had a look like maybe I would turn out okay after all. To be clear, they did not make me feel ashamed for any part of my life. My parents accepted me how I was.

In high school I had cut out words from a magazine and taped them to my mirror. They said, "Nothing but the truth." I dreamed of being a writer, but not just any writer — a writer of truth. In college, I took a couple journalism courses but had a nudge to change direction. I stopped attending college in my second year due to financial reasons and lack of clarity on what I really wanted to do. I prayed for guidance while working as a waitress in a locally-owned restaurant in Annapolis, Maryland.

Before long, I came across an ad in the local paper for a school in Baltimore focusing on the healing arts. I felt this was the answer to my prayer. Shortly after enrolling, I found out my aunt Nancy had just enrolled in the same school, and we would be attending some of our classes together. During this time I got to know my aunt and we became close. We both graduated in March of 1998, and I worked as an independent contractor for a year. Shortly afterwards I started a practice and have been in business ever since.

5

The Pursuit of Happiness

"Life, liberty and the pursuit of happiness" is a well-known phrase in the U.S. Declaration of Independence. I wanted to create a life of true freedom and happiness, but I did not know how. I spent my late twenties setting goals which I thought once achieved would make me happy. As I achieved my goals I still felt something was missing. I could not figure out what it was and wondered if it was my sexuality which caused this, events from my childhood, or something else. All I knew was there was something missing. I decided to hire a life coach, went to self-improvement seminars, and had a couple mentors. I read spiritual books and anything else I could think of to have a sense of peace and happiness, of success.

Deep down I feared being gay because at some point I started to wonder if it was an affront to God. I had heard this off and on throughout my life. In one of my college classes the teacher had us debate whether homosexuality was a choice or not, whether it was right or wrong, and if so, on what basis. I listened to some compassionate arguments for people loving someone of the same sex, and then I listened to some points to the contrary. When it was my turn I gave my debate points about as dryly as Ben Stein's character from the movie "Ferris Bueller's Day Off." There was no way I was outing myself by passionately explaining why they should have compassion for same sex couples. It wasn't worth it. My heart ached to have peace. I felt like a woman dying of thirst in a waterless desert. It is difficult to be close to God, to yourself, or anyone else when you have walls around you for any reason. I am responsible for putting up these walls, but I had no idea how to get them down. They were built brick by brick with expectations of how my parents should have behaved, as well as expectations of how I should be.

Eventually I realized I was carrying some shame. This was part of the problem but not all of it. A friend of mine shared with me how self-destructive shame can be from a book she read. The author basically says shame declares, "I am something wrong" where guilt says, "I did something wrong." There is a big difference because if we feel guilty we can make a change if we choose to, but when we take on shame we cut ourselves off from love by saying, "I am not worthy." I realized this was why I felt so distant from God at times and maybe it was why I could no longer have flying dreams. I often wondered if I would ever be able to experience the spiritual freedom of leaving my body again. I wondered if I <u>did</u> something wrong and wondered if I <u>was</u> something wrong. The fear of going to Hell for being homosexual was like a record playing in the back of my mind. Sometimes it was on a low, subtle volume and sometimes it was loud. As much as I would love to say I sought God for more noble purposes, early on in my seeking I just wanted to find out for myself, once and for all, does God really love me just as I am? All of me?

I was in need of healing. Accepting myself just as I am in this lifetime and getting to a point where I could be comfortable in my own skin was no easy task. It took nothing short of many healings from God. The healings did not end in me renouncing my sexuality as some "religious experts" might suggest. It ended in me making a conscious choice to live my life without concern for the opinions of others. I now know without a doubt that God loves all Souls regardless of whom they choose to love. If my life brought me nothing more than the capacity to love another Soul more than myself then I have not lived in vain.

6

Boxes and Labels

A box is a mental construct the mind uses to categorize, sort, and label. This is useful to some degree, but it is detrimental to ever going deeper in knowing God, others, or ourselves. When we think we understand something mentally we label it, put it in a box, and stop contemplating on it. In other words, we shut down to "the more" that is always there. Everything in God's Creation is growing or evolving in some way. This includes our understanding of God, ourselves, and others. When we put people in boxes we do not give them the freedom to be who they truly are, and when we do this to ourselves the result is the same. I cannot control how other people see me, but the more I do not label myself the freer I am to continue to grow into the real me. Soul is the real me and is eternal and boundless so it cannot be put into a box. Although I share experiences later in my story where I was taken to the Abode of God, what I share are attributes of God and aspects of Soul that were shown to me. My viewpoint is what I could accept at the time — it is by no means a complete definition.

I know my parents did the best they could. Even if they had been "perfect parents" I still came into this world with my unique lessons to learn, and they were the perfect Souls to help me learn them. In my mid-twenties, my father mailed me a heartwarming letter declaring how awful he felt for his alcoholism and for the fights I saw between him and my mother when I was a child. He sincerely apologized, and within his letter he admitted to being ashamed of his behavior. I had no idea he was still carrying this with him. It softened my heart towards him, and I told him I forgave him and thanked him for what he did do for us. I was beginning to have more of an inkling how difficult it is to change now that I was older. When I was ten my middle brother Orion was born, and when I was twelve my youngest brother Colin was born. My father quit drinking when Colin was born. He had intermittent relapses throughout his life, but he finally came to the conclusion it was not worth it and gave up alcohol. Upon reading his letter I prayed he could forgive himself and move on. I did not want him living with that regret.

I grew up not being able to see my real image staring back at me when I looked in the mirror. All I could see was what I was not. Nothing seemed to make up for this label I had allowed on myself. I was a "lesbian." It finally stuck. I had forgotten about Soul, the joyful and real me that used to fly around as a child and have adventures in the night. The more I did what other people thought I should, the less confidence I had. I avoided situations that could cause emotional pain or rejection. If I was in a social setting I was usually anxious so I drank alcohol to relax and be more "myself." The more I said yes to things I really did not want to do, the harder it became to say no. Some may think it is unusual for someone with relatively good looks to lack confidence, but to me it makes the case that until we have a "true self-image" we don't have what I now consider real confidence. I was insecure and afraid to simply live truthfully. My slogan "nothing but the truth" had become a joke. I was not living my heart's desire, especially in being honest about my sexuality.

7

My First Love

God blessed me in my early twenties with my first love. We were together for eight years. This should have been a joyous occasion for me, but falling in love with someone of the same sex back then also meant hiding that love. There were a small handful of people with whom I shared this part of my life, and coming out was not easy. I had to admit to them I had been living a lie. I had been hiding this part of my life for years trying to appear "normal." Now with a chance for love, it was worth it to come out of hiding a little bit.

I moved in with my girlfriend Kim in 1994. Kim was a restaurant manager and a few years older than me, and what most people would consider successful. She and her friends worked in the corporate world while I was in the service industry. God gave me the perfect job to learn how to serve others and get over myself. I lived in Northern Virginia at this time and was employed in a higher-end restaurant where they had different rankings for the servers. The best servers were called "top guns" and they had the best shifts. Some made enough money to support their families. I was much younger, less experienced, and used to part-time shifts in small cafes and dives, so compared to them I was an awful waitress!

One day a fellow server said to me during Sunday brunch as I was on my knees picking up crumbs from a family of six, "You know this job is just one big lesson in humility, right?" I never forgot her words. At the time, I aspired to move on to a better job, but years later I realized I was learning to have the heart of a servant. In time I would learn of the beautiful attribute of humility which I had been sent to Earth to learn. One thing I learned from waitressing was my attitude could make or break the day. If I came in grateful to be working the day went smoothly and everything flowed. If I had a poor ungrateful attitude, someone was going to get something dropped on them, or I would have a slow shift and make no money. Having people to serve was the only way to make a living as a server. Those with a bad attitude were like repellant to the good tables and good shifts.

Kim's parents did not approve of same-sex partnerships, and she was afraid of disappointing them. If her parents came over she asked me to pretend to have my own bedroom and act like we were just friends. I suspected after many years her parents knew we were in a relationship, but they did not want to hear about it, so she did not tell them. Over time I stopped respecting Kim and eventually stopped respecting myself for not having the courage to tell the truth. Back then you could lose your job for being openly gay, and sometimes people called you names if you so much as held hands, much less danced in public. I understood why we were choosing to live secretly, but it still felt wrong to lie.

I had developed a pretty serious drinking problem by this time. I could say it was because of the shame, living a lie, or any other excuse — but the truth is I liked to drink. It had become a close companion to me, and although I rarely got drunk, I knew I drank too much. It was interwoven into anything I did. If we were going to have crabs by the Chesapeake Bay, we had beer. Going on a romantic date meant wine with dinner. Meeting friends after work meant martinis — you get the idea. Unraveling this habit was like pulling at a loosely knit sweater, soon I would be exposed and what would cover me? I felt I would be completely exposed and vulnerable without it. During this time in my life I felt I needed it for managing stress and having fun. It reminds me of a bumper sticker I once saw that said: "Beer is proof that God loves the Irish!" For me it was similar.

Kim and I eventually broke up which was better for both of us. I am grateful for the lessons our relationship brought and for her love, but negative opinions from our relationship lingered in my mind. I did not feel good about myself, and I was trying to prove to the world I was good enough so I bought a lot of stuff. I bought a condo on a golf course, and I soon realized I don't even like golf. I bought nice clothes, watches with certain names which symbolized status, and a nice car. I wanted to convince myself and everyone else I was "successful and happy." I wanted Kim's parents to have a better opinion of me even though I would never see them again. Fancy stuff was pretty opposite from who I really was, but I figured the opposite of who I was had to be the better version. It makes me think of a *Seinfeld* episode back in the nineties where George decides to do everything opposite from how he normally does it, and suddenly his life goes perfectly. Jerry Seinfeld called this version "Opposite George." Opposite me was not working. It seems silly now to think I allowed myself to be controlled by other people's opinions of me, but I did at one point.

The breakup with Kim was a turning point for me. I was now in my late twenties, and I wanted to get myself together and be ready if another opportunity for love came around. I decided I was not going to live in hiding anymore, no matter what. I made notes of the things I wanted to change and started to see a life coach. I bought books on financial planning, I attended self-improvement seminars regularly, and I went to a couple AA meetings. At one meeting, the speaker directed us to step three, which consisted of turning our life over to our Higher Power. At the time this concept was a bit unsettling to me. I was under the impression I had control over alcohol. But he assured us until we did this we would not be able to quit. It sounded plausible, but I did not want to quit just yet. It's kind of like when you know the answer to what you should do, but you keep stalling by "praying on it" some more. I was doing this.

8

A Higher Love

My aunt Nancy and uncle Paul had given me a dream journal as a birthday gift around the age of twenty-seven and shared something very precious with me. It was HU, a love song to God which can be sung quietly to oneself or out loud with the eyes closed. In time, I started to remember more dreams especially on nights when I sang HU before bed. I started writing my dreams down and reviewing them for insights from time to time. I asked for God's help in my life, and I could tell things were changing in a positive direction.

One day I attended a seminar in Washington, DC just after my twenty-ninth birthday and made a friend. Also in her late twenties, her name was Jodi and she was from Florida. We went out from time to time and she introduced me to new friends, which I needed since the breakup. She called me on a Sunday evening after dinner and invited me to go out. I normally did not go out on work nights, but I sensed I needed to go for some reason. I went with her to a softball meeting at a local bar in DC. This is where I met Shanna. She was wearing a casual outfit of jeans, a baseball jersey, and tennis shoes, but she may as well have been wearing a ball gown. I was stunned the moment I saw her. We started talking and became instant friends. We set up our first date a few nights later and began dating regularly thereafter. We had a long-term relationship (with a brief breakup), which eventually led to marriage twelve years later when it became legal.

I was really grateful to meet Shanna. Through her I began to realize that all those things I was trying so hard to be I already was. In her eyes there was no distance between all my goals and me. I was good enough just as I was. She saw the real me, as Soul. It would be many more years before I saw it for myself. Shanna was stable in every sense of that word. God's Love flowed effortlessly from her. Gentle, strong, and wise, she was outwardly beautiful to me, yet what I saw was radiating from within. Her love inspired me and uplifted me. I would not be where I am today without her example. She is one of the most genuine people I have ever known, and I consider myself blessed to be her wife.

After dating for about six months we went on a vacation to the Virgin Islands together. The vacation went great, but she seemed too good to be true. I allowed what other people thought to override my gut instincts. I had a life coach at the time and she advised me just before our vacation that Shanna was too young for me. I was turning thirty and Shanna was just turning twenty-three. I did what the life coach thought I should, which was end the relationship before I got too far into it. Lesson learned. All consultants are just that. I now take their advice into consideration but follow my own heart. The day I broke up with Shanna I knew I had made a mistake. My stomach was in knots, and I could not get over how I felt. I prayed to God for guidance and decided to sleep on it. For not knowing someone very long, I was surprised by how difficult our breakup was. The next day I had a strong sense I needed to try to make up with her. I called several times but she never answered. I knew she was avoiding my calls. I finally left a message for her to call me back. Later in the evening she called me. I prayed for a sign so I would know if she was "the one." During our phone discussion Shanna shared a dream with me that was the answer to my prayer. After she shared the dream I knew she was someone I had known in a prior life. Years later I found out we had indeed met before.

9

Shanna's Dream

Before falling asleep that night, Shanna prayed for a spiritual guide to comfort and help heal the hurt in her heart from the breakup. A peace-filled Soul appeared to her in the dream state. I was in the dream with her, and we were in a place filled with light. This peaceful Soul seemed to be a spiritual master. He showed her past lives we had been in together, and she saw the possibility of a future life together as a married couple. He instructed us to turn and face one another. "See one another as I see you," he said. As we looked into each other's eyes our physical bodies faded away, transforming into brilliant light. All became light surrounding us yet we recognized one another. When Shanna shared this dream, I knew she was "the one." I asked her to forgive me. She did, and we started over with a new understanding of ourselves. We were not male or female really. We were two Souls who loved each other. This has always been part of the foundation of our relationship. Not knowing much about how to make a relationship work, I wanted to be a good partner for Shanna. Over time I wondered during contemplation, "What is love?" I began to see love is demonstrated. It is a verb, an action word. This heartfelt prayer and God's Grace led me to the Guidance for a Better Life retreat center.

10

Guidance for a Better Life

My aunt Nancy and uncle Paul had been attending retreats in Virginia at Guidance for a Better Life. At the time they lived in Edgewater, Maryland in a renovated cottage on the South River of the Chesapeake Bay, and I lived about fifteen minutes away in Crofton, Maryland. When I would visit I noticed each year they had a new group photograph from a retreat they called "Reunion." There were usually about fifty students gathered for the picture taken outside with a background of beautiful green trees early in summer. Their teacher Del was always seated on a bench somewhere in the center of the picture with his wife beside him. Curious, I asked questions. "What do they teach at the retreat center? Why do you keep going back?" I didn't imagine there was so much to learn about nature. Soon I discovered it was a spiritual school, and students were learning more about their Divine nature and the nature of God. It seemed whatever spiritual endeavor I had tried Nancy would imply there was more. Finally, I had to find out for myself what this "more" was, so I asked Shanna if she would like to go and we applied for a retreat. Our applications were accepted and we arrived at the retreat center a month later on a rainy spring day. Our first visit was thick with fog on the mountain so I did not have a clear view, but the subsequent retreats were more sunny and clear, and I noticed more detail with each one. We were high up on a mountain in Virginia and the view was different from here. There is something beautiful about looking out from a higher view. Perhaps the fog during my first visit represented metaphorical scales being lifted from my eyes. I seemed to have greater clarity with each visit to the mountaintop. Funny enough the awareness I was getting revealed just how unaware I was about God, my motivations, and my surroundings in general. But hope was also offered like a cup of water to a weary traveler. I could do this!

The most noticeable feature of the property was a deep-water pond, which on clear days sparkled in the sunlight as gentle breezes stirred surface ripples. Water from the pond poured into the outlet stream and flowed down through the property and beyond. Shortly after we arrived and put our belongings in the sleeping shelter, Nancy took us to meet Del and his wife Lynne. Nancy escorted us to the school building where Lynne happily greeted us with a hug. She said she was glad we made it, and her presence was comforting and reassuring. She had a way about her that made you feel at ease. Lynne has been a beautiful example for me over the years of what it means to give love and service to God in a way that is all her own. Her example inspires me in subtle, but life-transforming ways. Something as simple as bringing her husband a cup of coffee with a grateful smile has been for me a discourse in grace and love. She often had a good joke ready to open our hearts with laughter before Del would begin teaching.

Here at my first retreat I finally met the man I had seen in a photo many years prior on my aunt Nancy's refrigerator. I finally met Del Hall III, the spiritual guide qualified to raise me up to a higher way of life. When I met Del I was awkward and shy around him. Something about his presence made me feel an excited anticipation. I don't know how to describe this, but in his presence I felt inwardly stirred. Perhaps the real me as Soul recognized him. He was different than anyone "religious" or "spiritual" I had ever met. He was not in either of those boxes.

There was something special about him, but I did not know what it was. I found out during retreats Del also had a wonderful sense of humor which was like a soothing balm on my anxiety. His jokes were not what I expected, but they spoke to my heart, awakening joy once stifled by the stuffiness of what other "spiritual people" were like.

This is what I needed. Del's students always get exactly what they need when they need it. I had a mental box, based on my past experiences, of what I would have to be like in order to be pleasing to God. I wasn't sure I could completely conform to the box I had in my mind, but I was willing to try to martyr my sense of humor to gain God's Love and approval. Now I breathed a sigh of relief because by Del's example, it appeared I could be "spiritually enlightened" while still having fun. I had faulty visions of what God expected of me and of all the ways He might expect me to prove my love for Him. These images grew to be sacrificial and torturous, something I could never really acheive. These were misconceptions I had picked up from lifetimes past and this current lifetime. For me there was a seriousness, a heaviness associated with the responsibility of being "godly." It stood in my way, stealing my joy, and hindering me from time to time. Fortunately, I have been given bite-sized pieces of help with this over many years since my very first retreat in 2004.

I wanted to know more about Del and our possible connection, so I asked for dreams while at retreats and at home on several occasions. He would appear in my dreams teaching me. I thought this was interesting. Never before had a teacher come to me in a dream. I later learned that God's Prophets and His authorized spiritual guides can come to teach us in dreams. They can also take us to God's Temples of learning within the inner planes which are traveled as Soul. I had to admit this was certainly more than what I had ever seen at any other retreat I attended. Del was teaching spiritual freedom: the ways, truth, and path home to God. Being invited to come to Guidance for a Better Life and be a student of Del's was the answer to my lifelong pursuit of true happiness and freedom. It is here I would learn about God's Love for Soul through actual experience, not simply from scripture. Here I would continue on my journey into the Heart of God, literally traveling spiritually with Del to meet my Heavenly Father.

Del shared HU with us, an ancient name and love song to God. He explained that singing HU is a way to "tune into the God channel." This made sense to me. As I explained earlier, HU was shared with me prior to coming to the retreat center by Aunt Nancy and Uncle Paul. The first time I sang it in a group I wept. It awakened something deep inside and the eternal part of me was crying tears of joy. My heart was opening and walls were crumbling down. Perhaps this is one of the first healings I received from God while singing HU. It has become an integral part of my daily life, and I cherish this blessing.

"God's truth does not need to be embellished," Del said during one of the discourses at a retreat I was attending. One of his students was trying to be poetic in explaining their experience. The experience was amazing on its own, and embellishment by man only diminished its true beauty and muddied its purity. Del helped us to see if we were not being honest with ourselves, or if we were confused about an experience, it could potentially damage a student listening or the person sharing if not clarified. He is all about truth, which is rare indeed. This was a refreshing change from other teachers in my past. Del said we all have "truth detectors," which I had never heard before. This sounded right, and it felt good to hear someone name it. A truth detector is like a built-in instinctive knowing on whether something is true or not. Some of the experiences students were blessed with could sound impossible or preposterous, so we had to rely on more than our minds to know what was true and what was not. I invite you to do the same as you consider my experiences. Real knowing is beyond mental knowledge or the mind — it is a part of our Divine inheritance as Soul.

At the last self-improvement workshop I took in DC around 2003, prior to coming to Guidance for a Better Life, the instructor said something I knew was not truth. He was being very forceful and pushy at the very end of the course with what he was saying, insisting we accept it and go out and do it. I stood up and called "B.S." Several other students agreed with me, but the teacher simply tried to brush it off as our misunderstanding of his statement. He told me he wondered what was on the other side of my resistance. I later found out the answer — Guidance for a Better Life! I decided that was my last class. I had learned what I could there and left with a sense of gratitude and also a sense of strength.

When hearing Del teach I was reassured he spoke truth, not his version of truth. Many people had tried to tell me there was no right and wrong and no truth, there was simply our interpretation of the truth. I realize there are many sides from which something can be viewed. At times in my seeking I was told I was being too black and white and there was a lot of grey area. Perhaps in some cases, but not when one is looking for God literally and not metaphorically. I was looking for someone who could share God's truth. I knew I was finally where I was supposed to be. A peace settled into my heart after this. Parts of my journey would not be easy, but I was where I was supposed to be. I made a note in my journal not to forget this.

At my first spiritual retreat we sat on handmade wooden benches in an open-air building overlooking the beautiful pond. There were no gold engravings and high-ceiled chapels with murals of angels. Del wasn't wearing a white robe with sandals or a fancy hat to announce his presence with authority, but I knew in my heart he was worthy of great respect. He was real. There was nothing phony about him or what he was teaching. I believe the people teaching me along the way had good intentions, and I did learn some life lessons which were helpful. Each teacher I had was appropriate for where I was at the time.

Although my intentions were to improve in some way, "self-improvement" is a bit of an oxymoron. There is a fundamental difference in Soul and Self, which I learned at the retreat center. Del teaches his students how to operate as Soul, which for me worked more efficiently than constantly trying to stop bad habits or unwanted behavior patterns generated by the mind. With his teachings came an opportunity to be raised up in consciousness. I did not even know this was possible, but I was experiencing glimpses of my true self, Soul, with each retreat I attended. I was being raised above the constant stream of thoughts jumbling through my mind. Many teachings I had tried claimed all kinds of results, but what I was left with after the dust settled was only a sensation. I had been entertained but was no more enlightened when I left.

11

The Blue Star

During one of my early retreats I had my first spiritual experience on the property. I headed to my tent when class was dismissed, prepared myself for bed, and shortly after going to sleep I awoke in my spiritual body for the first time since I was a child! I was outside of my tent lying on a large piece of flat mountain rock with Shanna. We were both in our Soul bodies made of shimmering light. I thought I was in my physical body at first glance because everything looked the same — it was so real. The stars were crystal clear in the night sky, and the moon shined brightly. As I gazed at the shimmering stars above me a holographic, three-dimensional image of a blue star emerged before my eyes. The star appeared, and a feeling of great peace and love began to build within me. It started in my heart and elevated up into my eyes. I could not touch this blue star, but I tried because it looked so real. As I reached for it my hands went through the image. I waved my hands in front of my eyes several times as I examined whether it was inside or outside of my mind. It seemed to be in neither place, so vivid, alive, and majestic. As I did this I recalled how earlier in class Del had shared that the inner presence of God's Prophet can come as blue light, and I knew "The Star" was Prophet's presence. The inner Prophet was introducing himself to me. I felt so much love coming from him.

As we lay on the rock, still awake in this dream gazing into the night sky, Shanna and I began a discussion about a past-life we had together. We were casually talking about a lifetime where we both knew each other. She was sharing with me how much she loved trains, and how she liked a particular

Christmas ornament on top of our tree. Enough detail was given that I found out we were young brothers around the ages of nine and twelve, and she had died unexpectedly from typhoid fever. We were both sick at the same time, but I recovered and she did not. As we were talking I felt a surge of emotion and a heavy sensation near my chest, a mixture of sadness and illness.

I realized as a gift of love Prophet had taken me out of my physical body and allowed me to experience myself as Soul. Prophet showed me what it would be like to have no physical body, perhaps like upon the time of death. He showed me it is possible to travel spiritually and come back to the physical body without dying. I experienced myself as Soul, my eternal self which had no fear of death. I did not view death or aging the same after this experience, because I was shown we do not really die and love does not die. I recall this experience untangling me from some long-held fear of loss of loved ones.

Shanna and I had been reunited in this lifetime, and the revelation of this was deeply touching and healing. If you have ever had someone pass on to the other side before you do it can be very sad. Even if you believe you might see them again, the pain can stay with you. In my case, it was still with me from almost one hundred and fifty years ago. Sadness I was carrying, which I was not even consciously aware of, lifted from me and also any fear or concern about death in general. I woke up from this dream experience renewed.

I thought God must love us very much if He would give us a spiritual guide capable of sharing love and truth in precisely the right way for us. Shanna and I are on individual spiritual paths, but together we are incredibly blessed to be here attending retreats together. I was aware in this moment of a prayer answered. I asked God years before coming to the retreat center, after Kim and I broke up, to bring me a partner who would love God, and who would make walking a true spiritual path a priority. God answered my prayer and then some! I looked out at the property just before awakening into my physical body and everything was translucent and glowed with white light. I had found something pure I had wanted for a very long time, longer than one lifetime would suggest.

12

My Blue Bead

Del offers us a special gift after some retreats which is a blue bead. The beads are very old and rare. They are difficult to find, and we take care not to break them as they are made of glass. Del explained although the beads are "just beads," and we are not into idolatry they are very special. I treasure this gift. The bead is a symbol to me of my experiences over the years. It is a symbol of how many lifetimes I have wanted the opportunity to meet a Prophet of God and have the chance to be a student.

It takes Soul many lifetimes to become refined enough to be in the presence of a teacher like Del and be teachable. Just as an infant would be wasting his or her time to apply for college without growing up and learning, so it is with Soul. Although I have always had an appreciation for my beads I am realizing how special they are on a deeper level. Yes, from one view it is "just a bead," however what is contained within the beads is priceless to me. I have several necklaces which have been made with love and care by Lynne. Throughout the day I find myself reaching for them. An instant knowing comes over me — I am Soul, a divine spark of God. I am never alone. God loves me. I am most fortunate and grateful every day to be able to appreciate life, even on the hard days. It reminds me there is always a silver lining and to look for it. It reminds me to trust in God, to focus on love but not to be naïve. To take responsibility for my life and to be the best steward I can be of the opportunity I have been given.

13

A Wind of Change

One summer evening as Del was teaching a weeklong retreat the electricity went out, and he went outside to have a look. A few minutes passed, and he came back in and asked if we wanted to come outside and look too. I stood up and exited the retreat center building we call the "Beach House." As I looked out the clouds had turned dark gray as lightning and thunder clapped from distant clouds. We watched in awe as a great wind and undeniable stirring permeated the air. There was a sound developing with the wind that was like a freight train as it built up momentum and came towards us. A lot of students began to work together to secure loose items which could blow away, such as chairs and pantry items for cooking. I could sense something significant was happening but I did not know what. Afterwards I seemed different in a positive way, like something was activated deep within me. I seemed to have more courage than before. I had more trust in God that I was safe in His care. My awareness of this inner shift came in waves throughout the year, not all at once that night.

Later that evening Shanna and I walked to the field where our tent was set up and saw that it was damaged. The wind had whipped it up and crashed it to the ground. A student commented that the wind was like "Pentecost" in the Bible, and she jokingly called what happened to several students' tents, "Tentacost." Although she was joking there seemed to be a similarity. A storm with great wind came from the Heavens, and I was changed by it. During the year after this event I realized Del had gotten a significant upgrade to his ordainment from God, becoming His Prophet after a short period of transition. What we each experienced personally was because of our relationship with him. He now had an even greater ability to help his students access their divinity.

As I looked out at the field where we had put our tent, I noticed not all of the tents had been destroyed. For me this was an awake dream, a communication from God of the urgency of moving from Maryland to Virginia — a move we had been considering. The tent represented my condo in Maryland. The destruction of the tent represented any equity I thought I might get from the sale of my condo. I had been delaying our move with the hope that the real estate market would get better, and my condo association would recover. Seeing the destroyed tent sent a message to me it would not get better, in fact it might get worse. I felt strongly we needed to move to Virginia now and not wait.

14

Moving from Maryland

At this time I had an established small business in Annapolis, Maryland. Leaving and starting over seemed daunting. I had a condo that I had been trying to sell for two years. The Homeowners Association was not getting enough dues because of the housing crash in 2008. This made the people who were paying their dues have to pay much more to cover the foreclosed properties. This made my home difficult to sell at current market value because the higher dues added another four hundred dollars per month to the cost of ownership. Over the years I had invested in improvements so I was attached to getting at least some of that money back. Instead of getting better it was getting worse. The dues kept increasing. Finally I went to my realtor and conceded that I would go ahead with a short sale and take a loss. I knew I needed to let go of this place and move forward. I wanted to be closer to Prophet both physically and spiritually. I had to let go of "the old life" and accept "the new life" God had for us.

It also became clear that I needed to quit drinking once and for all. During a solo at a retreat at the school I wrote a letter asking Prophet to help me be rid of my drinking problem. What once brought comfort and relief was now a wedge between God, His Prophet, and me. I did not send the letter, but I knew I had been heard. I surrendered the outcome and forgot about the petition for help. I never gave up trying to quit alcohol. I might have been considered a social drinker by many standards. By God's Grace I had cut way back, but still I knew drinking alcohol for me was like tuning into the negative channel rather than the God channel. I wanted to be tuned into Prophet and able to hear his valuable guidance. After all, why go to a retreat center to learn how to listen to God if you are going to continue to do something that blocks listening — it just seemed stupid.

We moved to central Virginia in 2012, and I worked hard to get my practice up and running like it had been in Maryland. My work is rewarding but physically demanding. I ran a special to gain new customers and doubled my workload to compensate for the decrease in pay. I was working too much, had poor boundaries, and allowed myself to become stressed out and out of balance. I could relate to the scripture (1 Peter 5:8 KJV) "Be sober, be vigilant; because your adversary the devil, as a roaring lion, walketh about, seeking whom he may devour." Although I was no Bible expert this caught my attention while flipping through channels one day as I cleaned the house. A preacher was giving a sermon and I happened to hear this part. It was a clear message! I was trying to do everything myself. I had asked for help inwardly but was not really trusting because I had anxiety. In a moment of weakness I drank again, breaking my promise to God and myself. I was very disappointed in myself but determined not to give up.

15

Breaking Out!

I had a dream while writing this book which illustrates the struggle of Soul to be free of the limitations of the little Self and the worlds of materiality in general. Once Soul is liberated we can help free other "captives" with our testimonies, spreading the teachings of God, sharing the love of Prophet, and "walking the talk" if we choose to. In this dream I was on a field trip with some fellow students at Guidance for a Better Life. We took an airplane, and when we arrived at our destination we entered a store which seemed futuristic and past all at the same time, and like a scene from just before the end of slavery in America. A black man was serving a group of aristocrats at a large wooden banquet table. They treated him poorly but he served them dutifully. In the next scene, I was in a box in the basement of a mansion and a vice was closing in on me from all sides. Just when I thought it was going to crush me it opened up and gave me a tiny space to move. This went on repeatedly. Finally I was tired of being in this enclosure and I decided to wiggle myself out inch by inch. It took a lot of time, patience, and effort. Once out, I heard the servant being thrown in a dungeon so I ran to help him.

Next, the scene got very dramatic, almost like I was watching the end of a movie. It was as if I were the servant in the dungeon and also watching the scene play out. The captive was played by the actor Will Smith. His actions were determined and purposeful. He was completely focused on getting out of this dungeon. Nothing else seemed to matter to him. There was straw loosely thrown about the dank dungeon, and he was smoking a cigar. He took the flame from the cigar, touching it to the straw and igniting the whole cell he was in. The flame soon engulfed him, and he screamed in pain, but the fire motivated him to get out. He turned as if looking into the movie camera, teeth gritting the cigar and said, "So help me God, I will not stay in here!" With everything he had in him, he busted through the dungeon and ran off to defeat his captors. And then I woke up from the dream.

This dream has multiple meanings so I am not going to interpret all of the possibilities, but the undeniable theme is a desire to be free. In my interpretation of this dream, each character represents aspects of myself. The field trip represents Soul reincarnating on Earth, the airplane represents another plane of existence, for example the physical plane. Will Smith represents willpower, which is good and useful to a point but not enough to bust free. The attitude of the prisoner stands out to me. In setting the prison cell on fire he can only go in one direction, forward. The attitude says, "I am going to get free or die trying." He literally breaks through a wall to get free. I do not mean to discourage anyone who is interested in spiritual freedom, but the dream is a perfect metaphor for the attitude it takes to get out of the gravity of the lower planes of existence. It takes proper instruction, practice, prolonged determination, focus, and a love for God and Prophet so great that it literally consumes you like a fire. The idea that we can ride into Heaven permanently on someone else's effort is simply untrue. We need to want it for ourselves, make our own effort, and persist for a very long time. Lifetimes, in fact. We also need help from the true Prophet of God because our own willpower is not enough. Thankfully God <u>always</u> has a chosen Prophet on Earth.

The day after this dream I was driving to take my dog hiking with me and I saw a license plate that said, "I'm Free." As I contemplated on these nighttime and awake dreams, I felt the message represented God's Mercy and Grace in my life leading me to a place where I am finally able to make conscious choices rather than be led around by impulse. This does not imply I never feel emotions like anger or fear. It means I now have a choice whether I want to stay that way. What a blessing!

To be clear, we do not break free only once. Just as I was in a tiny box in the basement and wiggled my way free, only to be put into a larger dungeon in this dream example, so it is with our growth. Living in a state of freedom is a process with relative degrees depending on our state of consciousness. For example, as a child I traveled spiritually, however I was limited to my backyard and the Astral plane which is slightly above the physical plane. With Prophet's help, I now have the ability by his grace to travel with him throughout the worlds of God.

This dream signified being set free from unconscious ignorance and choosing to use my free will to have a relationship with Prophet, polarizing myself towards God with better choices rather than staying in darkness through ignorance. One of the greatest gifts of spiritual freedom was learning that when Prophet shows me an aspect of my lower self it is a gift of love and not a judgment. Del's son said this at a retreat he was teaching and it resonated with me. I had viewed truth of this nature as a criticism, a sort of condemnation of who I would always be. With Prophet's help, these lower nature attributes take a back seat.

16

God's Chosen Prophet

Del Hall III was now the Prophet of our times, and I had the privilege to become a disciple during a ceremony held at a small class I attended in December 2012. You may be wondering how one becomes God's chosen Prophet. I do not profess to know the ways in which God chooses His Prophets, however I can say the spiritual mantle transmitted during the great windstorm affected a large portion of Virginia with downed power lines and quite a bit of destruction. The force which entered into this physical plane from the Heavens was not invisible. It was not a metaphor or figure of speech. It is real and is the power of the Word of God given to His Prophet. It descends and enters into the new Prophet at his initiation or rite. Del is authorized to speak for God and His ways, and he has told us he is always growing too. He is ever the humble example of walking God's ways and teachings.

Del kindly invited us to decide if we wanted to accept his offer to continue teaching us as God's Prophet. What a demonstration of respect for Soul. I would have thought it was a given we would all want to be his students, but he asked us and in so doing reminded us what he is here for primarily: "Do you still want to learn the ways of God, do you still want to go Home?" We gathered around him and sang HU, a love song to God. He took us spiritually upwards towards the highest Heaven where only light and goodness reside. Del, as the inner Prophet, held his hands out to me palms up, and I placed my hands in his palms down. Looking into his eyes I saw the brightest future emerge as I walked with him into a vista of light. This was to be my new life; a life lived in his spiritual presence. I saw myself surrounded in blue and gold light as I declared, "I will never let go of these hands!" Prophet would help me realize the dreams of my heart if I would make a continued effort. I accepted the invitation to be under his guidance and care. Words fail to convey what this means to me. This promise is something I relive almost daily. I have won the spiritual lottery of lifetimes! However, it is an opportunity for me, not a guarantee. I must never be complacent in this realization.

17

Surrender

While attending another weeklong retreat I had a dream which showed me more truth about my drinking problem; the opposition I had been struggling with for quite some time now. The message I got from this dream was that my attachment to this habit was an open door which would allow the thief to steal everything dear to me. I had a vision of where my life would be if I did not get over this obstacle. Although Prophet is here to help us achieve our dreams, the devil, or whatever name you wish to use for the negative power, is here to stop us from manifesting these dreams. He uses anything he can, mostly our Achilles heel and illusions. This is why knowing our lower nature is just as important as knowing our higher nature.

It is much like knowing your weaknesses in a sport or a war. If we know where we are weak we can strengthen and ask for help. If we are blind to our weaknesses they can be exploited and used to defeat us. The passions of the mind like vanity, addiction, greed, anger, emotional imbalances, and excessive attachments to materiality are highways for the negative power to put a wedge between us and God. Prophet helps remove those walls, but we must also be aware of the traps.

I did not volunteer to share the dream at the retreat because everyone had heard this issue before. I was sick of hearing about it, and I was sure the class was too. I had thought the problem was behind me. My uncle Paul, also a student of Del's, shared his dream in class which had me in it. Paul's dream put my dream into play. Del turned his attention to me. At this point I had been sober for six months, sincerely doing my best. I truly wanted to be free of this. Del knew my heart. Not knowing what else to do, I instinctively knelt on the floor in front of my chair exhausted with this issue. Inwardly I begged forgiveness with what seemed like lifetimes of guilt in my heart. I felt every part of myself opening to God. There was so much I had been carrying. I had no idea. I had never really "let go" until that moment. On my knees before the whole class, I finally surrendered. With the full power of God's mercy Del intervened on my behalf and broke the shackles of this addiction, washing away years of broken promises, regret, shame, and denial. I felt truly "reborn" after this. As I sat up from the floor I realized what I was thirsting for had been in front of me for years. I had looked at Del many times, but with this wedge removed it was as if I finally "saw" him. God's Presence poured through him, It's Divine channel. He is the water of life. It was as if a dam had burst around me, and my heart flooded with love for the Divine authority that flowed from him. This love flowed into my heart and back out to Prophet.

The act of kneeling in humility was something I had wanted to do in Prophet's presence. It had been building in me over the years, and when I finally had the opportunity to do it, it actually brought a sense of relief. This was a deep, Soul-knowing type of submission. Part of why I drank was because my lower self was infected with vanity and anxiety. I drank because it made me feel better. I was still all about me most of the time, even though I wanted to be a servant of God. I did not care how my actions affected others around me as much as I could have. I was unaware that how I behaved in the world around me mattered. I still thought I was an island, and my actions only affected me. Deep down I do not think I truly accepted that I matter.

God cares about me and God cares about those around me too. The self-absorbed and self-destructive nature of this habit began to become clear, and I developed a distaste for it that nurtures my healing to this day. I still have times when I get down on my knees and praise God for my sobriety because the memory of the desire is not something that just goes away magically. I have to be vigilant in my thoughts and thankful for my healing or I become vulnerable to this affliction. It is unreasonable to think I can be complacent, go to a summer barbeque, or pass by the many wineries and breweries I live around, and not sometimes have a memory of drinking. It happens, but I choose to remember the healing and the clarity of why I no longer drink. By God's Grace and my own commitment to my healing, I quit drinking December of 2012.

The inner Prophet helped me see how I had fallen into the same trap as my father. I now understood why my father had broken his promises to us so many times when I was a child. He would promise to stop drinking but he would always start again. At one time I was angry at him because he could not see how his actions affected us. Now I realized I had done the same thing. I now understood with compassion how difficult it is to overcome addiction. It can be the perfect vehicle to bring us to our knees, throwing up our hands in futility of our own puny efforts. This weakness for me became a strength. I was beginning to see how coming to God in weakness, asking for help, and gaining His strength was huge. When I truly surrendered in genuine humility I seemed to gain everything in that moment. An elevation in my understanding of who Del is and what he teaches came instantly. Love is not a big enough word to describe what I saw in His eyes, yet it was all this and more.

This moment was a big turning point for me. More and more moments like these have come in various ways over the years. Trials and mental cataclysms would give way to bright new vistas and higher views. This process is never-ending and comes again and again, each with greater depths of trust between God, Prophet and me. There was more healing to come, and now I was more receptive to the help I wanted.

The inner Prophet once showed me what it was like to have so much to give to someone who asks for my help, and then have them not trust me enough to do my job. I had a client like this and it was very frustrating for me. Not because the client would not do what I wanted her to, but because she wanted help and I had the tools to help her, but she was not receptive. I could see that her anxious nature and mistrust was not personal; it was likely from past experiences she was unconsciously bringing into her sessions with me. I had compassion for her struggle when I realized she was acting how I acted at times throughout my journey when Prophet tried to help me. This experience showed me how not every situation calls for gentleness, and not every situation calls for a more direct approach. Being free to do whatever is best for the client makes for the best sessions. Prophet has been given authority by God to help us in any way, but we are the limiting factor in how much of his blessings we receive.

18

A Healing HU

One summer day at the Guidance for a Better Life retreat center I experienced a retroactive healing while singing HU. I didn't ask for this. I just prayed to give all my love to God and receive whatever was given. I hiked to Vision Rock, which is a special place at Guidance for a Better Life where students go sometimes to contemplate or simply enjoy the view. I sat down on the rock and began singing HU. I invited the inner Prophet to join me. To my delight we traveled spiritually above space and time into past and future lives. I felt like I was traveling through a wormhole at the speed of light. Scenes flashed by as if we were in a speeding car.

I had an amazing experience and a healing that penetrated into the past, present, and future. We began to slow down at important areas where Prophet suggested I look. As we traveled I saw all of the places where I did not recognize God's Love. It was there but I had not noticed it. I was taken back to my childhood in this lifetime. I clearly saw my mother standing at the kitchen sink with her flower-printed apron on washing vegetables and praying over our food, hoping we would grow up healthy. I saw my father come through the door after a long day of work excited to share his day with Mom. I saw my brothers and me enjoying each other's company, sharing playful banter, and making forts in the house. I saw my father at some of my tennis matches in high school and college, cheering me on. I saw my mother walking my brother and me along a stream through the woods as young children.

Each of these moments was given to me as a gift from God. These were the precious childhood memories I had forgotten — the good memories. The memories erased all those years ago by disappointment, fear, anger, hurt, and never wanting to feel that way again. The memories erased by a wall of protection which became a prison. Inside this prison was the comfort of never being rejected because I would not take the chance to be hurt; I was never really "all in." Inside the prison was the safety of a very tiny space I thought I could control, but it had no love within it. God's Love was everywhere around it, waiting for the walls to come down. As my heart opened to feel love on a profound level, a healing occurred. The metaphorical prison began to dissolve. What I could see of God's Love appeared as a golden effervescent light gently nestled around each scene. It was soft and beautiful to look at. I was taken back thousands of years and then to the present moment, then into the future. I saw God's Love in every detail of my life, which was one continuous life lived as Soul within different lifetimes. I had male and female bodies. In some lives I was wealthy, in others I was poor or living a humble existence of everyday survival. I had been a wife, a king, a warrior, a son, daughter, and a husband. I had been many nationalities and races. I had been oppressed and had been the oppressor, had forgiven and wanted forgiveness. Through all of these experiences, I gained more wisdom and a greater capacity to love. Prophet showed me more of the eternal thread of my life.

19

Facing Fears

Even with all of these amazing experiences I realized I still had not faced a major fear. I had a question still unanswered I wanted to put a period on. The question was, "What if once I get to a certain point on the path God asks me to give up my relationship with Shanna?" We had been together for twelve years. We were not married yet, and I was still not sure deep down if God was okay with this aspect of my life. I kept wondering if God's will for me was to be with a man, and He was just waiting for me to be strong enough to do the right thing. I did not want to lose Shanna and loved her deeply, but I needed to know the truth once and for all. After mustering enough courage to accept whatever the answer was, I decided to give my relationship to God and I said: "Thy Will be done." If He wanted me to give it up I decided I would. In a small way, this act was for me like the story in the Bible of Abraham being willing to sacrifice his son. It turned out God did not want Abraham's son, but perhaps Abraham did not know that any more than I knew what God wanted from me. I found out He did not want my relationship, but when I knew I could give it up if it truly was His Will, I was free of the fear that had me. God wanted me free of this fear, and the act of giving my relationship to Him revealed a spiritual strength I had never before known. God did not want to take away "my stuff" or anyone I loved. In fact, He gave me my relationship back even more blessed than it had been. This act of surrender opened the door for my marriage to Shanna and brought more love for Prophet to the surface, which helped me experience vulnerability, a skill set of love I had not had the courage to try.

20

A Journey to Lemuria With Prophet

At an advanced retreat with a select group of students, Del offered an opportunity to travel spiritually to a place that existed during the ancient history of the Earth now long forgotten. As we sang HU and the spiritual name of Del when he was the Prophet during this time of Lemuria, a memory of having lived there emerged in my consciousness. Some may not even believe Lemuria was a real place, but I can testify it was indeed, and a great civilization of peace and harmony permeated the landscape. I was among one of the people inhabiting this beautiful continent surrounded by a great ocean.

As we sang his name a scene began to develop. There were tall mountains in the distance, an ocean, and lush tropical green plants all around. I could hear the sounds of insects in the background as the salty sea air flavored my senses, and a gentle breeze washed over me. The air was warm and slightly humid. I could see a village of grass hut-like structures. I was drawn to one particular man in the center of a circle of people. He was tan-skinned with dark shoulder-length hair. For a moment I was taken close up to his eyes. They were Del's eyes, and he was leading a gathering to give love and devotion to God. Del and the Prophet of Lemuria were the same Soul. The mood of the whole group was happy and vibrant. I could see love and reverence in people's faces as they listened to him speak and looked upon his countenance as if hungry for the next word he would utter.

The scene changed and I had a flash of Shanna and me standing beside the ocean shore here in Lemuria. I instantly recognized her although she had a different body and face. We were at our wedding in that lifetime. She was male and I was female. Children played in the distance and their laughter cascaded through my memory. Some were our children. So much love and joy surged through my heart. It was very strong and real.

In the next scene, we were in our Soul bodies in front of the manifestation of God's Altar. We were taken to God's Ocean, the twelfth Heaven, by Prophet. We were spiritually on our knees, exchanging vows with an aspect of God. We held out our right hands like one does when a ring is about to be placed on the finger. We were given rings of golden light that became a part of us. This light came directly from God into us. God's effervescent Light and Sound, alive with sparkling majesty, manifested as waves rolling onto the beach where we knelt and bathed us. We were nourished and given strength here at this Holy sanctuary of God. The touch of my true Father strengthened every weakness within me, and I knew my purpose: To be a servant of God, to accept His Love for myself, and to distribute it to others through my sacred relationship with Prophet.

As this experience came to a close, a blue light encompassed me and a sense of coming full circle, knowing I have never been alone, was made very clear. Perhaps the faces and personalities of God's Prophets have changed, and I had lifetimes when I was not consciously aware of this presence, but it has always been with me. This proved to me my relationship with Prophet is eternal, ancient, unshakable, and sacred beyond any doubt. Prophet wants to see us free and once the connection is made in any lifetime the love is always there.

21

An Ancient and Sacred Promise

Del as Prophet made a promise to me in that lifetime in Lemuria more than fifty thousand years ago he would find me again and take me back home to the Heart of God. I made a promise to him I would "wake up" spiritually and be receptive to his help. He promised me I would recognize his voice, his eyes, and his spiritual presence, and I would know him. Words cannot truly describe a relationship this special, but it is my hope that my sharing will give you as the reader a taste of how much God loves Soul, His child. He sends his Prophets to gather up ready Souls and escort them home to Him.

I was overcome when I realized this is no ordinary love. It is deep, beyond emotion, beyond anything I have ever known. Soul, the deepest part of me knows the truth of how long Prophet has watched, waited, and hoped for any spark of interest from me. He has cheered me on through my triumphs and comforted me through my trials. A prayer to know my own love for Prophet helps me overcome the fears and limitations of the little human self. It is more than a transformation; it is a transmutation. A transmutation is changing from one species to another. Being human means identifying with the limited lower nature. Being Soul means identifying with my God-like nature which is giving, and not self-absorbed. I still have much to learn, but I am grateful I am going through the process with Prophet, and I am so thankful I am not where I used to be. I enjoy giving service to God.

The Prophet Jesus told his disciples service is the reward. How long I have contemplated that simple truth, and how very long my heart has wanted to get it. Perhaps it is beginning. I am growing in love to be His servant, which is the greatest of all joys. This is what being taken to the Heart of God, while my physical body sat in a chair at Guidance for a Better Life, has done for me. It has revealed my true character and heart's desire. I now know why I was created and what my true purpose is. Being able to give and receive love is what I am here to learn, and marriage is helping to teach me more about this as I serve my wife and grow in my love for her.

July 18, 2015 is the day I was married to Shanna by Prophet Del Hall. A huge wall of shame came down for me, the doubt burned, its ashes scattered into a past-life, and the old me became like a distant memory. Going to the Heart of God meant being given His permission to love whom I choose. Our wedding was held outside on a hot summer day. As I looked out into the gathering of family and friends at what seemed like a vista of God's Light, I breathed in a sense of sanctified dignity blended with humility as I was escorted down the wedding aisle by Del. It was as if my Heavenly Father was walking me down the aisle, so happy to see me in love. I took my place at the altar and waited for my soon-to-be wife to join me. The love of God was evident and palpable in every way.

It was predicted to rain, but it only sprinkled briefly just before our ceremony. Spiritually I felt as if I was in a shower of God's golden Light which poured down all day long. I knew that many people, including Prophet, had wished us well and hoped for the best weather. We were surrounded by friends, children, family, and our closest loved ones on a day I will always cherish.

Prophet has always been with me in the ancient sense. His inner presence is with all of us all the time; it is omnipotent and omnipresent. It is a force we can begin to recognize with some effort, and being conscious of it in everyday life reminds us we are not alone. God truly does love us, but we have much to learn. I would not have learned much, and my story would not be very interesting if all it contained were pages of me on a puffy cloud sitting next to God, enjoying my existence with other Souls doing the same. The richness of adventure and the development of who I am as Soul is amazing. Doesn't it make you wonder who you might be as Soul? I wonder what lifetimes you might have known one of God's Prophets? Perhaps if you search your heart and ask for truth, a veil of illusion may begin to lift. This is ultimately what I am being healed of: illusions.

22

Getting Out of the Maze

In one of my spiritual study guides I came across the term "seekers of truth." I realized I was a seeker of truth before I came to the retreat center. When I was a young lady I had taped those words "nothing but the truth" to my mirror. The words were remnants of seeds planted by Prophets before. The definition of a seeker of truth is one who sincerely works at any sacrifice to attain truth. What I sacrifice is my little self for my true self, illusions for a more true reality. It is sort of like I was in a maze before I became a student of Del's. I was struggling to find my way out, hitting walls, finding dead ends, turning around, and looking for a better way. Being taught the ways of God by Prophet was like being given a ride in a helicopter, lifting me above the maze where I could see more of the big picture. I began making better choices for my life as he showed me the most direct route out of the maze. I felt like I had been through this maze enough times to know that without help I was not going to get out.

This is a rudimentary example of what it is like for Soul reincarnating over and over into the maze of life in the lower planes of God, hoping to one day find the One who can lead him out. Soul is naturally humble and interested in truth. Soul is excited to learn and does not assume it knows everything already. The little human self is not interested in truth because most of the time it thinks it already knows. What I am trading are the desires of the little self, the limitations of the little self. The petty ways of the human consciousness must be exchanged for the better way of God if one is to find their way out of the maze.

One of the goals of spiritual freedom is to allow Soul to be in the driver's seat while the mind is its instrument. The mind alone is not something to be revered, as many people do. It is actually quite a frightening sight to see the mind operating by itself without Soul's positive influence, much like a heavy machine without a driver careening about aimlessly. If you have ever struggled with worry, anxiety, or fear, this is the mind on autopilot. I have heard some people say, "I cannot contemplate. I do not have the patience or temperament." If you can worry you can contemplate. It is a matter of training and awareness. Learning to control my subjective little self is a key to spiritual freedom. If my daily life is run by anxiety, anger, addictions, insecurities, and the like, I am not free to any degree. If I am the effect of what other people think of me, the boxes they put me into, I am not free. I am learning how to let go and grow in my love for God, for His Prophet, and myself. I am learning to grow in my love for Soul and God's creation. You are Soul, and as such can be happy, at peace, and have the ability to experience boundless joy. Spiritual freedom is truly having the freedom to utilize your God-given gift of free will. It is having the freedom to experience Divine love, to give it and to receive it.

23

Diamonds Made to Shine

What I have learned is everything is spiritual and potential grist for the mill of life if I can learn and grow from it. If I can somehow be a little better today than I was yesterday in my ability to give back to life and be in tune with Prophet, I am happy. Del gave us a great example of how he helps us achieve spiritual freedom over time. He is like a master jeweler who has a diamond in the rough. First we yield to the process of spiritual growth. Eventually, if we recognize Prophet's eternal love for us, we can submit ourself. Once this is done he can begin cutting away the outer crust, which allows us to reflect God's Light, and our own light, like a diamond. We can begin a process of learning to operate as instruments for God, distributors of His Love. As a master jeweler cuts facets of a diamond, Prophet carefully chisels away the parts of my life that do not serve a purpose anymore. I owe my very life and happiness to God. I did not truly have life in the real sense until His Prophet agreed to teach me the ways of God. He teaches me, once the least of His servants, how to be a true servant of God every day. It is by God's Grace I share my experiences with you in the hopes you will know God loves you, and God always has a Prophet to help us find our way back home to Him. You are worthy of God's Love!

So, what is left when the outer crust is chiseled away? I am still finding out, but I can tell you of a nakedness, a willingness to be vulnerable with God, which grows and gives me the most sanctified sense of freedom and security. What I am left with is the absolute knowing that my life is in the Hands of God, and if I continue to nurture and build the sacred relationship I have with Prophet, my splendor as Soul is limitless. I am left with a sense of optimism and less concern over worldly affairs which pass by like a parade, because no matter what happens on this Earth — it will pass. No matter what labels man uses to define God, I know there is always more. There is more to us than what we see in the mirror, more than what we have been telling ourselves, and more than what others have told us. God will not be put into a box, love will not be put into a box, and I will not be put into a box! I have discovered that those who pursue life, liberty, and happiness in the truest sense can find it. Look always for the one who holds the keys. Look for God's Prophet!

Postscript

One Life, Many Lifetimes

To really understand my story it is important to understand the perspective from which it is written. First, I have lived more than one lifetime, which I shared in my story, but I have one eternal life as Soul. This is true for everyone. Soul is an individualized piece of the Holy Spirit made of God's Love, which is His Light and Sound. While living on planet Earth Soul wears a type of "earth suit" which consists of the body and mind. Similar to how astronauts use a space suit on the moon, Soul requires a specialized suit or protective covering while residing on Earth.

There are distinctions between Soul, which I consider my true self, and my lower self which consists of my physical body and mind. The lower self is perishable, unlike Soul which is eternal and boundless. Compared to Soul the lower self is very limited.

The mind and body are intended to be used as instruments for Soul rather than define who we truly are. In other words we are Soul, we do not have a Soul. The lower self can be the effect of vanity, greed, fear, anger, addictions, and excessive attachments. These are like "road dirt" on a nice car. They are not permanent fixtures on the car and can be washed off. Sometimes these hangups inhibit us from experiencing God's Love and our own Divine nature. Soul is free to experience joy, peace, love, happiness, and continuous access to the wisdom of God. We are not at liberty to operate as Soul until the mind is trained to be subordinate to Soul by a teacher adept at such. Soul incarnates into many physical bodies throughout Its eternal existence.

Similarly, we can drive many different cars in our life and not identify as the car; we know we are the driver. Ideally, our lives are best run by Soul, but the lower self is a strong influence on Soul and it takes extensive conditioning to accept enough of God's Light to allow Soul to finally be in charge. This Light is distributed by God's Prophet. Long before I consciously recognized Prophet's spiritual presence in my life I had experiences, which looking back, suggested he was always with me.

What is Spiritual Freedom?

There are many types of freedom: financial, physical, emotional, belief, speech, and more. Freedom from what *exactly* is the goal of spiritual freedom? Basically, unconscious ignorance. It may be offensive to some readers to suggest that what Prophet offers us is an opportunity to stop being so ignorant. But think about it. How many times have you looked out at someone else doing something you thought was ignorant and thought, "If they only knew better." With great love and compassion God sends us His Prophets to help us make better decisions. Perhaps the wisest decision we can make is to have a conscious relationship with him. This is accomplished through moving into higher states of consciousness or awareness, which Prophet helps us do.

Consider with me a long view and a short view of life for the illustration of this point. A long view would be looking at our life from the perspective that we have lived many lifetimes as Soul. Within those lifetimes we have made decisions which shaped not only the future of that life, but future incarnations. We could call this "past-life karma." With this in mind, our genetic, cultural, and social position in the world today would be a reflection of our choices.

Soul might come into a healthy body or a sick one, a high intellect or with a mental disadvantage depending on past-life karma, and an assortment of lessons which are designed to help bring about spiritual maturity. In the long view, God's purpose for placing Souls in the lower worlds is not so much a punishment but a learning opportunity. With spiritual maturity comes humility, compassion, and a greater freedom to love God, love our neighbor, and love ourselves, which is stated in the Bible as the first and second great commandments of our Heavenly Father. (Matthew 22:37-39 KJV)

The short view would be looking at life from the perspective that we have one lifetime and we end up where we are based on luck or random circumstance. The color of our skin, whether we are born into a male or female body, and whether we are born into the favored country of that time period are random. If we are born into wealth or poverty, our particular family unit, and more is all circumstantial. With this one lifetime view it is easier to take on the victim role, where as with the multiple lifetime view it is easier to take responsibility for our choices and do our best to move forward once we know better. It has been my experience that being accepted as a student of God's Prophet teaches one to view life from the long view. It gives one the ability to make conscious decisions rather than decisions based solely on emotional reaction, logic, or survival instincts. Del explained to us, "Decisions are the exercise of free will given to us by a loving God." With this I realized it is a privilege to use free will, and that not every Soul exercises this freedom equally. Freedom is variable depending on our state of consciousness. For example, a prisoner in a cell has some freedom to make decisions, but it is very limited compared to someone living outside of the prison.

Summary of Useful Tools and Contemplations

It is important to note you do not have to find the outer Prophet to benefit from some of the teachings expressed in this book. You can sing HU, sending love and appreciation to God, and invite the inner Prophet who is always spiritually with you to come more fully into your life to guide you.

Of all of the ways to experience God's Love, the simplest is to look for it, it is all around. Next is being grateful. We have so much to be grateful for, and too often we choose to focus on the things we wish were different rather than noticing and being appreciative for the gift of life and the many blessings offered each day.

One of the many ways we can receive guidance is by asking for or praying for dreams. I started by simply using a journal, flashlight, and pen. I put them by my bedside table. I sang HU then asked God to show me love and truth. I surrendered the outcome and went to sleep. If I remembered all or any parts of a dream I wrote it down. I looked for patterns of behavior, symbols or recurring themes, and asked again in the morning for any insights what God wanted to communicate to me. It is a process, so be patient with yourself and know God hears you. In time you will hear Him.

Del shared a helpful tool early on that I still use today. Throughout many scriptures we are told God loves us. I like to affirm this. I find it especially helpful to affirm during times if I doubt myself or am going through a difficult time: "God loves me. I am worthy of God's Love. I accept God's Love." I repeat it until I remember it is true!

Another way to experience more of God's Love every day is to pray to be a blessing to another Soul and wait to see how God might use you to be one. In time you will begin to understand God's language and notice His blessings even more. With this comes a more abundant life. If all of this seems a bit overwhelming, like the thought of living up to Jesus' example did for me at one time, simply start with one goal. You could ask something like, "Help me learn more about Divine love, perhaps ways to give it or how better to receive it." Contemplate on Divine love and become aware of what happens throughout your day. Before long you might be practicing some of the ways of God whether you know it or not.

Prophet, thank you for your love and protection, for sharing God's teachings with me, for taking me ever higher into the Heavens of God, and giving me a view of life which continues to leave me in absolute jaw-dropping amazement. I love you!

Guidance for a Better Life
Our Story

My Father's Journey

Prophet Del Hall III

God always has a living Prophet on Earth to teach His Ways and accomplish His will. My father, Del Hall III, is currently God's true Prophet fully raised up and ordained by God Himself. He was not always a Prophet, nor did he even know what a Prophet was, but God had a plan for him like He has for all of His children. Over many years through many life experiences, God had begun to prepare my father for his future assignment, mostly unbeknownst to him. Everything he experienced in his life from the joys to the sadness helped prepare him for his future role as Prophet.

My dad grew up in California and was a decent student but a better athlete. He received an appointment to the United States Naval Academy in Annapolis, Maryland where he later met my mother. They were married two days after he graduated and received his commission as an officer. After a short tour on a Navy ship deployed to Vietnam, he went to flight training school and became a Navy fighter pilot. While attending flight school in Pensacola, Florida he also earned a Master of Science Degree and had the first of his three children, a son. After flight school he was stationed in a fighter squadron on the East Coast, where he and my mom began investing in real estate, adding to their family with the birth of two daughters. Following this tour of duty he was assigned as a jet flight instructor in Texas, after which, his time in the Navy was finished. He was a natural pilot and loved his time in the sky, but it was time to move on.

So far in life he had no real concern for, or even thought much about God, religion, or spiritual matters in general. He lived life fully. He raised his family. He traveled. He invested and became an entrepreneur starting and growing highly successful businesses in diverse fields ranging from real estate to aerospace consulting. Years before however, a seed had been planted when God's eternal teachings were introduced to him in his late teens, and while it did not show outwardly, the truth in these teachings spoke to his heart. My dad might not have been giving much thought about God up to this point in his life, but God was definitely thinking about him and the future He had planned for him. Like an acorn destined to become a mighty oak, the seed that lay dormant in his heart would someday be stirred to life. Through all his life experiences, both "good" and "bad," God would be preparing him for his future role as His Prophet.

When God decided it was time, He called my dad to Him. He did this by shutting down the world of financial security my dad had built. Over a period of two years all of his businesses were wound down and dissolved. What seemed like security turned out to be an illusion. Financial success had not provided true security. He now had failed businesses and a failing marriage and was trying to fix things without God's help, principles, or guidance. As painful as this time in his life was, it was yet another step towards the glorious life of service awaiting my father. God was removing him from the world my dad had created and furthering him along his path to his future role as Prophet.

After his marriage ended and his businesses wound down, he started fresh by going out west to give flying lessons near Lake Mead, Nevada. While living in Nevada my dad was reintroduced to the eternal teachings of God he first learned of as a teenager twenty-three years earlier, and though they resonated with him at the time, his priorities were different back then. Now, his serious training could begin. He started having very clear experiences with the Holy Spirit and noticed there was a familiarity with these teachings and experiences. He embraced the long hours of instruction, which often lasted until sunrise, and was receptive to the personal spiritual experiences he was given. This began an intense period of study and desire for spiritual truth that continues to this day. Some of his most profound and meaningful experiences during this time were with past Prophets of old. They came to him spiritually in contemplations and dreams. He learned of their roles in history and how they were raised up and ordained by God directly. He began to realize they were training him but was not clear why. A few times his experiences led him to believe he was in training to be a future Prophet. However, that revelation made no sense to him because he felt he was an imperfect person who made mistakes and had failures. He thought of the past and current Prophets of God as perfected Souls, not imperfect like he felt he was. Why would God choose him for such a role? He did not feel qualified.

Besides being introduced to God's teachings while he was out west, my father was blessed to meet his current wife Lynne. Returning to the East Coast, my father and Lynne moved into a small cabin on land he had acquired before his businesses shut down. This was a major change in his life, but it felt deeply right within him. He began to remember a desire to live like this as a child; from early childhood my dad found clarity and peace in nature. He had forgotten about this until now, but God had not and made this dream a reality. In addition to being their home, these beautiful, three-hundred-plus acres of land in the Blue Ridge Mountains would eventually become the location for the Guidance for a Better Life retreat center. The perfection of my father's experiences from earlier in his life in real estate, providing the land for his next step in life, speaks to the perfection of God's plan. One of many many examples I could list.

For many years my dad took wilderness skills courses around the country. He specialized in the study of wild edible and medicinal plants, tracking, and awareness skills, and authored articles for publication. Inspired to help folks feel more comfortable in the outdoors, my dad and Lynne began the Nature Awareness School in 1990.

Classes were focused on teaching awareness and the primitive living skills needed to enjoy the woods and survive in them if necessary. An amazing thing happened within those first few years though; students began to experience aspects of God in very personal and dramatic ways. Somewhat like my dad's experience out west, they found that stepping away from their daily routine and the hustle of life, if even for a few days, created space for Spirit to do Its work. Whether they were enjoying the beauty of the Virginia wilderness and tranquility of the school grounds or relaxing by the pond, he found students' hearts opened, and they became more receptive to the Divine Hand that is always reaching out to Its children. More and more the discourse during wilderness classes shifted to the meanings of dreams, personal growth, finding balance in life, and experiences the students were having with the Voice of God in Its many forms. An increase of spiritual retreats was offered to fulfill the demand and over time became the predominant class offerings; the wilderness survival skills classes eventually fading away completely. The name "Nature Awareness School" seemed to be less fitting for what was actually being taught now and in February 2019 my father changed the name of the retreat center to Guidance for a Better Life.

Throughout this time my father's training and spiritual study continued. My father reached mastership and was ordained by God on July 7, 1999 but he was still not yet Prophet, more was required. On October 22, 2012, twenty-five years since his full-time intensive training had begun, God ordained him as His chosen Prophet, and He has continued to raise him up further since. God works through my father in very direct and beneficial ways for his students. Hundreds and hundreds of students for more than thirty years have received God's eternal teachings through my father's instruction and mentoring. They have had personal experiences with the Divine which have transformed and greatly blessed their lives. My father's greatest joy is being used by God as a servant to share God's ways and truths with thirsty Souls and hungry seekers. In addition to mountaintop retreats, my father continues to spread God's ways and teachings that so greatly blessed his life and the lives of his loved ones in many ways, including his books and videos.

Maybe you are at a turning point in your life and looking for direction. Maybe you have a knowing there is more to life but not sure what that might be or how to find it. Or, maybe you are simply drawn to what you read and hear in our stories. God speaks to our hearts and calls each of us in many different ways. Like my father's journey demonstrates, it doesn't matter where you started or the twists, turns, or seeming dead-ends your life has taken; God wants us to know Him more fully, and for us to know our purpose within His creation. He wants us to experience His Love regardless of our religious path or lack thereof. He always has a living Prophet here on Earth to help us accomplish His desire for us — to show us the way home to Him and to experience more abundance in our lives while we are still living here on Earth. God's Prophet today is my father, Del Hall III. You have the opportunity to grow spiritually through God's teachings which Prophet shares. His guidance for a better life is available for you — please accept it.

Written by Del Hall IV

My Son, Del Hall IV

My son, Del Hall IV, joined Guidance for a Better Life as an instructor after fifteen years of in-class training with me, his father. He helped develop the five-step Keys to Spiritual Freedom Study Program and

Del Hall IV

facilitates the first two courses in the program: Step One "Tools to Recognize Divine Guidance" and Step Two "Understanding Divine Guidance." Del also teaches people about the rich history of dream study and how to better recall their own dreams during the Dream Study Workshops, which he hosts around the country. He is qualified to step in and facilitate any of my retreats should the need arise.

Del authored the book *God is in the Garden*, a priceless book of wisdom in the form of parables. Through stories of everyday events of life on the mountain Del shares profound insights into the nature of God and life that are infused with his natural humor and unique perspective.

Del is also Vice President of Marketing and helps with everything required to get the "good news" from Guidance for a Better Life out to hungry seekers: everything from book publishing, blogging, and posting on social media outlets. He is co-author and book cover designer for many of our, thus far, twenty published books.

My son loves the opportunity to work on creative projects for Guidance for a Better Life. From a very early age he has been an artist and loved creating artwork in multiple mediums. He was accepted into gifted art programs in Virginia Beach, Virginia and then after high school graduation he attended the School of the Museum of Fine Arts in Boston. He is now a nationally exhibited artist and his *Paintings of the Light and Sound of God* are in over two hundred public and private collections. One of the greatest joys of the painting process for Del is using his paintings as an opportunity to share with others the inspiration behind them, God's Love and his experiences with the Light and Sound of God, the Holy Spirit, in contemplation and in waking life.

Del lives on the retreat center property in the Blue Ridge Mountains of Virginia with his wife where they raised and homeschooled my three grandchildren. Recently he helped me with an extensive renovation and update for the three hand-built log cabins on retreat center property originally used for advanced spiritual retreats. He loves woodworking, tending to his vegetable garden, pruning his fruit trees, and helping maintain the beautiful three-hundred acres of retreat center property for students to enjoy. There is always something that needs attention on the land and Del is always up to the challenge. He loves to travel and spends his free time enjoying this beautiful country with his family in their RV.

My son has had multiple brain surgeries starting when he was seventeen years old for a recurring brain tumor. He credits God for surviving and thriving all this time when most with his condition do not. He looks to the sunrise every day with gratitude for yet another chance at life. With that chance he desires to help me share the love and teachings of God that have so blessed our lives. I pray to God daily thanking Him for my son's good health.

Written by Prophet Del Hall

What is the Role of God's Prophet?

An introductory understanding of God's handpicked and Divinely trained Prophet is necessary to fully benefit from reading this book. God ALWAYS has a living Prophet of His choice on Earth. He has a physical body with a limited number of students, but the inner spiritual side of Prophet is limitless. Spiritually he can help countless numbers of Souls all over the world, no matter what religion or path they are on — even if that is no path at all. He teaches the ways of God and shares the Light and Sound of God. He delivers the living Word of God. Prophet can teach you physically as well as through dreams, and he can lift you into the Heavens of God. He offers protection, peace, teachings, guidance, healing, and love.

Each of God's Prophets throughout history has a unique mission. One may only have a few students with the sole intent to keep God's teachings and truth alive. God may use another to change the course of history. God's Prophets are usually trained by both the current and former Prophets. The Prophet is tested and trained over a very long period of time. The earlier Prophets are physically gone but teach the new Prophet in the inner spiritual worlds. This serves two main purposes: the trainee becomes very adept at spiritual travel and gains wisdom from those in whose shoes he will someday walk. This is vital training because the Prophet is the one who must safely prepare and then take his students into the Heavens and back.

There are many levels of Heaven, also called planes or mansions. Saint Paul once claimed to know a man who went to the third Heaven. Actually it was Paul himself that went, but the pearl is, if there is a third Heaven, it presumes a first and second Heaven also exist. The first Heaven is often referred to as the Astral plane. Even on just that one plane of existence there are over one hundred sub-planes. This Heaven is where most people go after passing, unless they receive training while still here in their physical body. Without a guide who is trained properly in the ways of God a student could misunderstand the intended lesson and become confused as to what is truth. The inner worlds are enormous compared to the physical worlds. They are very real and can be explored safely when guided by God's Prophet.

Part of my mission is to share more of what is spiritually possible for you as a child of God. Few Souls know or understand that God's Prophet can safely guide God's children, while still alive physically, to their Heavenly Home. Taking a child of God into the Heavens is not the job of clergy. Clergy have a responsibility to pass on the teaching of their religion exactly as they were taught, not to add additional concepts or possibilities. If every clergy member taught their own personal belief system no religion could survive for long. Then the beautiful teachings of an earlier Prophet of God would be lost. Clergy can be creative in finding interesting and uplifting ways to share their teachings, but their job is to keep their religion intact. However, God sends His Prophets to build on the teachings of His past Prophets, to share God's Light and Love, to teach His language, and to guide Souls to their Heavenly Home.

There is ALWAYS MORE when it comes to God's teachings and truth. No one Prophet can teach ALL of God's ways. It may be that the audience of a particular time in history cannot absorb more wisdom. It could be due to a Prophet's limited time to teach and limited time in a physical body on Earth. Ultimately, it is that there is ALWAYS MORE! Each of God's Prophets brings additional teachings and opportunities for ways to draw closer to God, building on the work and teachings of former Prophets. That is one reason why Prophets of the past ask God to send another; to comfort, teach, and continue to help God's children grow into greater abundance. Former Prophets continue to have great love for God's children and want to see them continue to grow in accepting more of God's Love. One never needs to stop loving or accepting help from a past Prophet in order to grow with the help of the current Prophet. All true Prophets of God work together and help one another to do God's work.

All the testimonies in this book were written by students at the Guidance for a Better Life retreat center. It is here that the nature of God, the Holy Spirit, and the nature of Soul are EXPERIENCED under the guidance of a true living Prophet of God. Guidance for a Better Life is NOT a religion, it is a retreat center. God and His Prophet are NOT disparaging of any religion of love. However, the more a path defines itself with its teachings, dogma, or tenets, the more "walls" it inadvertently creates between the seeker and God. Sometimes it even puts God into a smaller box. God does not fit in any box. Prophet is for all Souls and is purposely not officially aligned with any path, but shows respect to all.

YOU can truly have an ABUNDANT LIFE through a personal and loving relationship with God, the Holy Spirit, and God's ordained Prophet. This is my primary message to you. Having a closer relationship with the Divine requires understanding the "Language of the Divine." God expresses His Love to us, His children, in many different and sometimes very subtle ways. Often His

Love goes unrecognized and unaccepted because His language is not well known. The testimonies in this book have shown you some of the ways in which God expresses His Love. It is my hope that in reading this book, you have begun to learn more of the "Language of the Divine." The stories spanned from very subtle Divine guidance to profound examples of experiencing God up close and very personal. After reading this book I hope you now know your relationship with God has the potential to be more profound, more personal, and more loving than any organized religion on Earth currently teaches.

If you wish to develop a relationship with God's Prophet, seek the inner side of Prophet, for he is spiritually already with you. Few are able to meet the current physical incarnation and most people do not need to meet Prophet physically. Gently sing HU for a few minutes and then sing "Prophet" with love in your heart and he will respond. It may take time to recognize his presence, but it will come. The Light and Love that flows through him is the same that has flowed through all of God's true Prophets.

A more abundant life awaits you,

Prophet Del Hall III

HU — An Ancient Name For God

HU is an ancient name for God that can be sung quietly or aloud in prayer. HU has existed since the beginning of time in one form or another and is available to all regardless of religion. It is a pure way to express your love to God and give thanks for your blessings.

Singing HU (HUUUUUU pronounced "hue") serves as a tuning fork with Spirit that brings you into greater harmony with the Divine. We recommend singing HU a few minutes each day. This can bring love, joy, peace, and clarity, or help you rise to a higher view of a situation when upset or fearful.

Articles of Faith

Written by Prophet Del Hall III

1. There is one true God who is still living and active in our lives. He is knowable and wants a relationship with each of His children. He is the same God Jesus called FATHER and is known by many names, including Heavenly Father, and the ancient names for God, HU, and Sugmad (Pronounced SOOG-mahd). God wants a loving, trusting, personal relationship with each of us, NOT one based upon fear or guilt.

2. The Holy Spirit is God's expression in all the worlds. It is in two parts, the Light and the Sound. It is through His Holy Spirit God communicates and delivers all His gifts: peace, clarity, love, joy, healings, correction,

guidance, wisdom, comfort, truth, dreams, new revelations, and more.

3. God always has a chosen living Prophet to teach His ways, speak His Living Word, lift up Souls, and bring us closer to God. God's living Prophet is a concentrated aspect of the Holy Spirit, the Light and Sound, and is raised up and ordained by God directly. His Prophet is empowered and authorized to share God's Light and Sound and to correct misunderstandings of His ways. There are two aspects of God's Prophet, an inner spiritual and outer physical Prophet. The inner Prophet can teach us through dreams, intuition, spiritual travel, inner communication, and his presence. The outer Prophet also teaches through his discourses, written word, and his presence. There is no separation between the inner and outer Prophet. Both inner and outer aspects of Prophet are concentrated aspects of the Holy Spirit. Prophet is always with us spiritually on

the inner. Prophet points to and glorifies the Father.

4. God so loves the world and His children He has always had a long unbroken line of His chosen Prophets on Earth. They existed before Jesus and after Jesus. Jesus was God's Prophet and His actual SON. God's chosen Prophets are considered to be in the "role of God's son," though NOT literally His Son. Only Jesus was literally His Son. Prophets were sometimes called Paraclete. The Bible uses the word Comforter, but the original Greek word was Paraclete, which is more accurate. Paraclete implies an actual physical person who helps, counsels, encourages, advocates, comforts, sets free, and more.

5. Our real and eternal self is called Soul. We are Soul; we do NOT "have" a Soul. As Soul we are literally an individualized piece of God's Holy Spirit, thereby divine in nature. As an individual and uniquely experienced

Soul you have free will, intelligence, imagination, opinions, clear and continuous access to Divine guidance, and immortality. As Soul we have an innate and profound spiritual growth potential. Soul has the ability to travel the Heavens spiritually with Prophet to gain truth and wisdom and grow in love. Soul exists because God loves It.

6. We have one eternal life as Soul. However, Soul needs to incarnate many times into a physical body to learn and grow spiritually mature. Soul's long journey back home to God where It was first created encompasses many lifetimes. A loving God does not expect His children to learn His ways in a single lifetime.

7. Soul equals Soul, in that God loves all Souls equally and each Soul has the same innate qualities and potential. Soul is neither male nor female, any particular race, nationality, or age. When Soul comes into a physical body at birth, the physical body is

male or female, a certain race, a nationality, and has an age. All Souls are children of God. We do not have to earn God's Love; He loves us unconditionally.

8. Soul incarnates on Earth to grow in the ability to give and receive love and learn to live the way God wishes us to live. Because God loves us, His ways of living create abundant, happy, fulfilling lives. His beautiful ways of living are mostly HOW to live, and less on what NOT to do.

9. God is more interested in two Souls learning to love one another regardless of their sexual preference. God loves you just the way you are.

10. It is God's will that a negative power exists to help Soul grow spiritually through challenges and hardships, thereby strengthening and maturing Soul. We are never given a challenge greater than our ability to find a solution to or understand the

necessary lesson, if we use our God-given creativity, make sufficient personal effort, and ask for and accept the help available from the Divine. Soul has the ability to rise above any obstacles with God's help.

11. We study the Bible as an authentic teaching tool of God's ways, in addition to books and discourses authored by a Prophet chosen by God. We know the original biblical writings are sometimes misunderstood, for example, God loves each of us regardless of our errors and shortcomings. God's eternal abandonment or damnation is not true. He would never turn His back to us for eternity. (Isaiah 54:7-8 and 10, Lamentations 3:31-32, and Hebrews 13:5)

12. Karma is the way in which the Divine accounts for our actions, words, thoughts, and attitudes. One can create positive or negative karma. Karma is a blessing used to teach us responsibility.

13. A child is not born in sin, however, the child does have karma from former lives. Karma, God's accounting system, explains our birth circumstances better than the concept of sin.

14. A living Prophet, including Jesus, can remove karma and sin when necessary to help us get started or to grow on the path home to God. However, it is primarily our responsibility to live and grow in the ways of God, thereby not creating negative karma and sin.

15. There are four commandments of God in which we abide: First — Love God with all your heart, mind, and Soul; Second — Love your neighbor as yourself. The Third is, "Seek ye first the Kingdom of God, and His righteousness." This means that it is primarily our responsibility to draw close to God, learn His ways, and strive to live the way God would like us to live. God's Prophet is sent to show His ways. Our purpose, the Fourth

Commandment, is to become spiritually mature to be used by God to bless His children. Becoming a coworker with God through His Comforter is our primary purpose in life and the most rewarding attainment of Soul.

16. All Souls upon translation, death of the physical body, go to the higher worlds, called Heavens, planes, or mansions, regardless of their beliefs. The way they live life on Earth and the effort made to draw close to God impacts the area of Heaven they are to be sent. Those who purposely harm others (except in defense of self or others), themselves, or live against the ways of God go to unpleasant locations on the first Heaven; to a location where they can learn how to do better, as a gift of love. The first Heaven has a wide range of locations, from very very unpleasant and hellish, to wonderful and beautiful places to spend time with loved ones while learning and preparing

for future incarnations. Those who draw close to a Prophet of God, including Jesus, receive special care. We know of twelve distinct Heavens, not one. The primary Abode of the Heavenly Father is in the twelfth Heaven, known as the Ocean of Love and Mercy. We can visit God while we still live on Earth, if taken by His chosen Prophet and only as Soul, not in a physical body.

17. Prayer is sacred, personal exchange with God and is an extreme privilege. God hears every prayer from the heart whether or not we recognize a response. Singing an ancient name of God, HU, is our foundational prayer. It expresses love and gratitude to God and is unencumbered by words. Singing HU has the potential to raise us up in consciousness making us more receptive to God's Love, Light, and guiding Hand. After praying it is best to spend time listening to God. Prayer should never be rote or routine. We desire to trust God and to know His will for us, and

then freely and joyfully surrender to His will rather than our own will. God's Prophet can teach us the "Language of the Divine" which will help us understand how God communicates with us and help us recognize God's Love in our lives.

18. It is our responsibility to stay spiritually nourished. When Soul is nourished and fortified It becomes activated, and we are more receptive and have clearer communication with the Divine. When Jesus said, "Give us this day our daily bread," he meant daily spiritual nourishment, not physical bread. The Holy Spirit is nourishment for Soul. This can be received by singing HU, studying Scripture, praying, dream study, demonstrating gratitude for our blessings, being in a living Prophet's physical presence or in his inner presence, or listening to his words.

19. TRUTH has the power to improve every area of our lives, but only if understood, accepted, and integrated into our lives.

20. God and His Prophet guide us in our sleeping dreams and awake dreams as a gift of love. God's Prophet teaches how to understand both types of dreams. All areas of our lives may be blessed by the wisdom God offers each of us directly in dreams.

21. Gratitude is extremely important on the path of love. It is literally the secret of love. Developing an attitude of gratitude is necessary to becoming spiritually mature. Recognizing and being grateful for the blessings of God in our lives is vital to building a loving and trusting relationship with God and His chosen Prophet. A relationship with God's Prophet is THE KEY to everything good. This includes a more abundant life filled with the Treasures of Heaven Jesus taught about in Matthew 6.

22. We are to be good stewards of our blessings. We recognize them as gifts of love from God and make the effort to have remembrance. Remembering our blessings helps to keep our hearts open to God and builds trust in God's Love for us.

23. We give others the respect and freedom to have their own beliefs, make their own choices, and live their lives as they wish. We expect the same in return.

24. The Love and blessings of God and His Prophet are available to all who are receptive. If one desires guidance and help from Prophet, ask from the heart and sing "Prophet." He will respond. One does not need to meet Prophet physically to receive help because he is a concentrated aspect of God's Holy Spirit, and is always with us. To be taught by Prophet in the physical is a sacred blessing. Much can be gained by reading or listening to the Heavenly Father's teachings being shared by Prophet.

25. We have a responsibility to do our part and let God and His Prophet do their part. This responsibility brings freedom. Our goal is to remain spiritually nourished, live the ways of God, live in balance with a core peace, and serve God as a coworker through His Comforter. We pray to use our God-given free will in a way that our actions, thoughts, words, and attitudes testify and bear witness to the Glory and Love of God.

26. There is always more to learn and grow in God's ways and truth. One cannot remain the same spiritually. One must make the effort to move forward or risk falling backward. To grow in consciousness and love requires change. Spiritual wisdom gained during our earthly incarnations can be taken to the other worlds when we translate, and into future lifetimes, unlike our physical possessions that remain in the physical.

Contact Information

Guidance for a Better Life is a worldwide mentoring program provided by Prophet Del Hall III and his son Del Hall IV. Personal one-on-one mentoring at our retreat center is our premier offering and the most direct and effective way to grow spiritually. Spiritual tools, guided exercises, and in-depth discourses on the eternal teachings of God are provided to help one become more aware of and receptive to His Holy Spirit and the abundance that awaits. With this personally-tailored guidance one begins to more fully recognize God's Love daily in their lives, both the dramatic and the very subtle. Over time our mentoring reduces fear, worry, anxiety, lack of purpose, feelings of unworthiness, guilt, and confusion; replacing those negative aspects of life with an abundance of peace, clarity, joy, wisdom, love, and self-respect leading to a more personal relationship with God, more than most know is possible. We also offer our videos, and more than twenty inspirational and educational books.

Guidance for a Better Life
P.O. Box 219
Lyndhurst, Virginia 22952
(540) 377-6068
contact@guidanceforabetterlife.com
www.guidanceforabetterlife.com

"A Growing Testament to the Power of God's Love One Profound Book at a Time."

If you could only read one of Prophet Del Hall's books this is the one. It is full of Keys to unlock the treasures of Heaven and bring more of God's Love into your life.

Wayshowers are God's special emissaries to Earth. Our Heavenly Father loves us so much He has never left us alone without a Wayshower to teach us His true ways. This book explores the amazing history of God's chosen and ordained Wayshowers from thirty-five thousand years ago to today through specific examples of both well-known and little-known Wayshowers.

GOD IS IN THE GARDEN
PARABLES

Regardless of what your venture is in life you can benefit from this unassuming book. It may appear small, but the parables contained within have the power to affect your life in extraordinary ways.

ZOOM WITH PROPHET

Guidance for a Better Life retreat center has been hosting in-person mountaintop retreats at our beautiful location in the Blue Ridge Mountains of Virginia since 1990. When the pandemic began in 2020, it inspired us to get creative with how to connect with our students and new seekers. It was then our *Zoom With Prophet* meeting series was born. Some of these Zoom meetings are now being put into book form for those who could not attend.

SPECIALIZED TOPICS

Whether you wish to reconnect with a loved one who has passed, understand how you too can experience God's Light, improve your marriage, or learn how to understand your dreams, these incredible books have you covered.

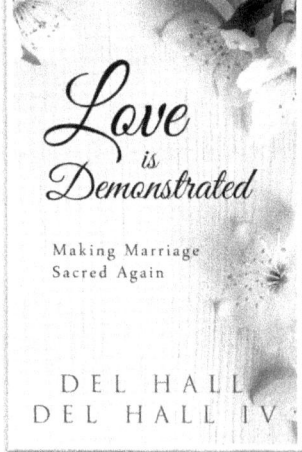

TESTIMONIES OF GOD'S LOVE SERIES

God expresses His Love every day in many different and sometimes subtle ways. Often this love goes unrecognized because the ways in which God communicates are not well known. Each of the books in this series contains fifty true stories that will help you learn to better recognize the Love of God in your life.

JOURNEY TO A TRUE SELF-IMAGE SERIES

This series includes intimate and unique stories that many readers will be able to personally identify with, enjoy, and learn from. They will help the reader transcend the false images people often carry about themselves — first and foremost that they are only their physical mind and body. The authors share their journeys of recognizing and coming to more fully accept their true self-image, that of Soul — an eternal child of God.

www.ingramcontent.com/pod-product-compliance
Lightning Source LLC
Chambersburg PA
CBHW071502040426
42444CB00008B/1455